SCIENCE VIEW

FORCES & MOTION

©2005 by Chelsea House Publishers, a subsidiary of Haights Cross Communications.

A Haights Cross Communications ⌐ Company

Printed and bound in China.
10 9 8 7 6 5 4 3 2 1

Library of Congress Cataloging-in-Publication Data applied for.

ISBN: 0-7910-8211-3

Chelsea House Publishers

2080 Cabot Blvd. West, Suite 201
Langhorne, PA 19047-1813

http://www.chelseahouse.com

Produced by
David West 👫 Children's Books
7 Princeton Court
55 Felsham Road
London SW15 1AZ

Designer: Gary Jeffrey
Editor: Gail Bushnell
Picture Research: Carlotta Cooper

PHOTO CREDITS :
Abbreviations: t-top, m-middle, b-bottom, r-right, l-left, c-center.

Front cover - br - Corbis Images. Pages 3 & 18b, 6 both, 8, 9, 11, 12t, 12–13, 17 both, 22t, 27 -Corbis Images. 7t, 16 both, 19, 20–21 - Rex Features Ltd. 10, 25 - Digital Stock. 10–11 - Katz Pictures. 12b - The Culture Archive. 24r - Robert Harding Picture Library.

Every effort has been made to contact copyright holders of any material reproduced in this book. Any omissions will be rectified in subsequent printings if notice is given to the publishers.

With special thanks to the models: Felix Blom, Tucker Bryant and Margaux Monfared. Also to The Clock Clinic.

An explanation of difficult words can be found in the glossary on page 31.

SCIENCE VIEW
FORCES &
MOTION

Steve Parker

CHELSEA HOUSE
PUBLISHERS
A Haights Cross Communications Company

CONTENTS

INTRODUCTION

Today's world never seems to stop. We are always on the move, racing from place to place. We have vehicles and mechanical equipment all around, and our buildings are packed with whirring devices and automatic gadgets. All of these depend on force, motion, and the science of mechanics.

How it **WORKS**

These panels explain the science behind the projects, and the processes and principles that we see every day, but which we may not always understand!

PROJECT PANEL

The projects are simple to do with supervision, using household items. Remember–scientists are cautious. They prepare equipment thoroughly, they know what should happen, and they *always* put safety first.

Are you moving as you read this? It may not seem like it, but you are. Over 300 years ago, the great scientist Isaac Newton worked out this, and much more.

The universe is in motion as stars swirl around in clusters called galaxies, and galaxies fly away from each other at unimaginable speeds.

LOTS OF MOTION

Sitting still in a chair, are you moving? Yes. You may be in a car, train, or plane. But even if you are not, you are on the Earth's surface, which moves as the planet spins around. Also, the Earth speeds through space at 18.6 miles (30 km) every second, on its yearly orbit around the Sun. And the Sun, Earth, and other planets whirl around the center of the galaxy at an incredible rate.

Clack! When one ball hits another, the movement, or kinetic energy, is passed on. The second ball speeds up and begins to move while the first one slows and stops.

MOVEMENT AS ENERGY

Our idea of movement depends on whether it is us or something else in motion–that is, motion is relative. Movement is also a form of energy, called kinetic energy. This energy can pass from one object to another,

Isaac Newton

or be changed into other types of energy, such as heat or electricity. Isaac Newton (1642–1727) worked out how and why movements occur, as shown on the following pages.

How it WORKS

Forces push or pull and alter the motion of an object. Newton's first law of motion says that an object will stay still, or keep moving with constant speed and direction, unless a force affects it. The force could be a physical knock or an invisible magnetic force.

Magnetic force

The ball bearing continues in a straight line unless a force acts on it. The unseen magnetic force pulls or attracts the iron-based steel of the ball bearing, making it swerve.

FORCED TO CHANGE MOTION

You can test Newton's first law of motion by making a shallow slope. Roll a steel ball bearing down and see how it travels in a straight line. Then put a powerful magnet nearby and roll the ball bearing again.

The nearer the magnet, the more powerful its magnetic force on the ball bearing, and the more the ball bearing moves toward the magnet. The steeper the slope, the faster the ball bearing rolls, and the less it moves toward the magnet.

Ball bearing

Strong magnet

Slope

APPLYING FORCE

A force, like a strong push, can make an object speed up or slow down and change direction, as shown on the previous page. However, in which direction, and by how much? Newton had the answers.

BIGGER OBJECT, MORE FORCE

It is easier to stop a golf ball rolling slowly than a basketball rolling rapidly. The force needed depends on the ball's mass (the amount of matter it contains, which is similar to the weight), and its speed. So, for the same force, a lighter object will be affected more than a heavier one. And for the same object, a large force will change the object's speed more than a small force.

Since a weightlifter's bar and weights have so much mass, they take a great force to get them moving as they are lifted from the floor. They have a large inertia.

FEEL THE FORCE

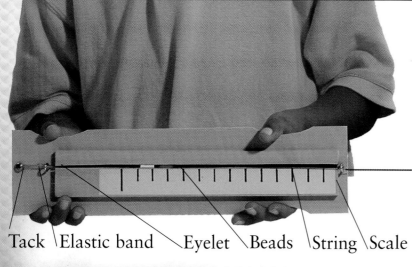

Tack Elastic band Eyelet Beads String Scale

Make a simple spring balance as shown above.

More mass means more inertia. You can show this using a toy truck, a spring-type weighing balance, and several weights. Tie the balance to the truck with string. On a level surface like a floor or large table, pull the balance gently while watching the pointer on the balance.

Note the reading at which the truck just starts to move. Put a weight into the truck. Pull the balance and again note the pointer reading as it begins to roll. Do the same with two weights, then three, and so on.

DIRECTION OF FORCE

When an object is affected by a force, it moves in the direction of the force. So, if the force is opposite to the object's motion, it slows the object down, and if it comes from the side, it pushes the object to the other side. The amount of change in direction depends on the object's mass and the force's strength. Newton set this out in his second law of motion.

A baseball has only 1/1,500th the mass of a batter. So, when the batter applies a force by hitting the ball with a bat, the ball changes speed rapidly and flies into the air. If the ball weighed the same as the batter, it would hardly move at all.

How it **WORKS**

Inertia is the tendency of an object to stay still, or, if it is moving, to keep moving with the same speed and direction.

As the truck and its load gain mass (become heavier), they have more inertia. So they need a greater pulling force to start them moving, as shown by the readings on the scale. Does the force increase by equal amounts, for the equal weights added to the truck?

Weights

Toy truck

"The starter flag falls, and they're off, trying to gain speed and take the lead!" Few vehicles and objects stay at a constant speed. They tend to adjust speed, going faster and then slower.

SPEEDING UP

When an object is stationary, a force is needed to make it speed up, or accelerate. If the force is taken away, the object stops accelerating. If the force continues, the object speeds faster and faster. Acceleration is measured as the increase in speed over a period of time, like one second. So, if speed is measured in feet per second, then acceleration is measured in feet per second per second.

A dragster is the ultimate acceleration machine, designed to go from stationary to as fast as possible over a short distance, like a quarter of a mile (400 m). Speeds exceed 300 miles per hour (483 km/h).

In sprint races, a good start is vital. This involves pushing off hard, to reach top speed quickly.

SLOWING DOWN

The greater a force, the faster an object accelerates. The longer the force continues, the greater the object's speed. Similarly, applying a force that opposes the object's direction of movement makes it slow down, or decelerate. Studying acceleration, deceleration, and the forces involved is important in many ways–especially for race-car drivers and astronauts, but in daily life, too.

Outer space is one of the few places where there are almost no other forces to counteract acceleration once it has started.

MEASURING SPEEDUP

Objects gain more speed on a steeper slope. You can study the link between acceleration and slope angle by using a toy cart, ramp, paper strips, and the top of a small plastic bottle filled with ink.

To make the cart as shown, use card, straws for the axles, and cotton reels for wheels. The slope and gauge are made from balsa wood. Make a hole in the lid of the plastic bottle. Put the ink in the bottle with sticky tape over the hole.

Position the cart at the top of the ramp. As you let go, pull the sticky tape off to let the ink start dripping.

Cotton reels

Drinking straws

Slope gauge

Card

Ink holder

Wheeled cart

Paper strip stuck to slope

How it **WORKS**

Ink should drip from the tiny hole at a constant rate, marking the paper. As the cart accelerates, it travels farther between each drip. The bigger the gap between the ink marks, the greater the acceleration.

Slower

Faster

When you lean on a wall, you apply a pushing force to the wall. Why does it not fall over? Because it pushes back with an equal force in the opposite direction. Newton knew this, too.

On a skateboard, you push off with your foot on the ground. This is the action. The reaction is the skateboard moving forward. How far you go depends on your mass and the force of the push.

TO AND FRO

Newton's third law of motion says that if one object exerts a pushing or pulling force on a second object, the second exerts an equal force back on the first. This is sometimes described as: "For every action, there is an equal and opposite reaction." Whether the objects actually move or not depends on their mass and how well they are fixed down.

The cannons on galleons were put on wheels so that when they fired a broadside, the ship was not tilted over by the recoil.

How it **WORKS**

When a cannon fires a ball, it recoils, or is pushed backward (reaction), with the same force as the ball is fired forward (action). It does not recoil as far as the ball goes, since it has a greater mass.

Action

Reaction

DOWN AND UP

One of the most spectacular examples of action-reaction is a space rocket. The rocket blasts hot gases downward with tremendous force. This has the effect of pushing the rocket upward with the same force, enough to lift an enormous craft like the space shuttle. Once in space, the rocket is pushed along by the gases shooting backward.

How it WORKS

The forces involved in a rocket taking off can be demonstrated with a simple party balloon. The air inside the balloon provides the pressure, or pushing force. When the air is finally released from the balloon, it shoots out downward. This is the action, and the equal and opposite reaction is the balloon shooting upward into the air!

Reaction

Action

The space shuttle craft, boosters, and fuel tanks weigh 2,204 tons (2,000 MT) at takeoff. The boosters give added force, or thrust, for the first two minutes, so the shuttle can break free of being pulled down by Earth's gravity.

13

Rub your hands together and they become warmer. This is an example of moving, or kinetic, energy being turned into heat energy, using force to overcome friction.

A Slowing-down Force

Any surface, no matter how smooth it seems, has tiny bumps and ridges. As two surfaces try to slide past one another, their bumps and ridges catch and snag each other, slowing the movement. Friction also occurs with liquids, slowing us down in water. It happens with gases, too, and slows objects speeding through air. This is called air resistance.

Car designers use wind tunnels to study aerodynamics, so they can create cars that have less air resistance.

A hovercraft has almost no friction with the ground, because it does not touch the ground. It rises on a cushion of air and floats along (see right).

FLOATING FRICTION-FREE

Air is slippery and flows easily, so a layer of air between two surfaces reduces friction. Push this hovercraft along when there is no air from the balloon, and again when there is air.

Carefully make a hole in the base of a lightweight plastic carton. It must be small enough for you to poke the balloon's neck in with a tight fit. Inflate a large balloon, then release the neck and quickly place the container on a tabletop.

FRICTION AS AN ENEMY

Friction is "the enemy of machines." In the moving parts of machinery, it converts movement energy into heat energy and can cause rubbing and wear, overheating, and loss of power. So, most machine parts are designed with smooth, hard, moving surfaces, to minimize friction. Slippery substances called lubricants, such as oils or greases, are used to lessen friction further.

Bearings are designed to reduce friction. Only small surfaces of the smooth ball bearings are touching when they are arranged in a circle.

FRICTION AS A FRIEND

Friction can be useful. Walking depends on friction between the soles of your feet or shoes and the ground. If there is little friction or grip, you slip over, as when walking on smooth ice. A vehicle's brakes also rely on it.

In motorcycle brakes, pads press hard on disks, creating friction, which slows the wheels down.

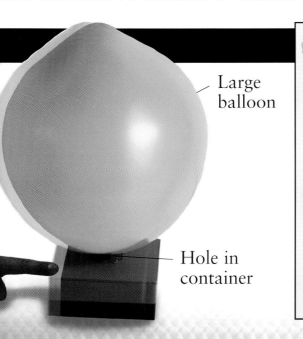

Large balloon

Hole in container

How it WORKS

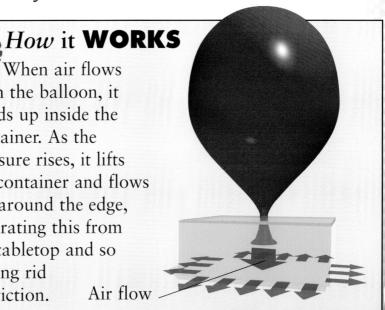

When air flows from the balloon, it builds up inside the container. As the pressure rises, it lifts the container and flows out around the edge, separating this from the tabletop and so getting rid of friction.

Air flow

There is one force we feel everywhere in the world– and it comes from Earth itself. It is called gravity and it pulls us and other objects down so we stay on the surface. But not only Earth has gravitational force–you have it, too.

Italian scientist Galileo Galilei (1564–1642) studied how fast objects fall under the force of gravity. He is said to have dropped them from the Leaning Tower of Pisa.

UNIVERSAL FORCE

Gravitational force is a feature of any object, anywhere in the universe–from a pinhead to a star. All matter or substance has it and pulls or attracts other matter. The force's strength rises with an object's mass (weight). The Earth is the biggest object in our daily life, so we feel its gravity strongly. The gravitational force of other objects, like cars or ourselves, is tiny by comparison and is rarely noticed.

How it WORKS

Legend says that Galileo dropped iron balls of different sizes from the top of the 177-foot (54-m)-high Leaning Tower of Pisa to show that all objects fall downward at the same speed. All objects accelerate under the force of Earth's gravity, g, at the rate of 32 feet (9.8 m) per second every second.

10lb weight

1lb weight

Astronauts on the Moon could jump higher than on Earth. This is because the Moon is much smaller and so its gravitational pull is only one-sixth that of Earth's.

Aircraft wings are more curved on the upper surface than on the lower, which creates a force called lift. It is strong enough to oppose the pull of Earth's gravity.

OVERCOMING GRAVITY

Gravity pulls things toward Earth's center. This is why objects fall down. To overcome it, so that objects can rise above the surface, there must be an opposite force that is stronger. Our leg muscles produce such a force briefly when we jump, but gravity takes over and we return to the Earth's surface.

HOW PLANES FLY

Planes fly by using an airfoil wing shape that is more rounded on top than below.

Handle

Fold a piece of paper in half. Push the top half forward, so the paper bows on top, and glue it in position. Make two of these wings. Make holes in the wings and join them by pushing straws through. Put threads through the straws and join at the base and handle as shown. Use a hairdryer to create wind.

Wing shape

Threads

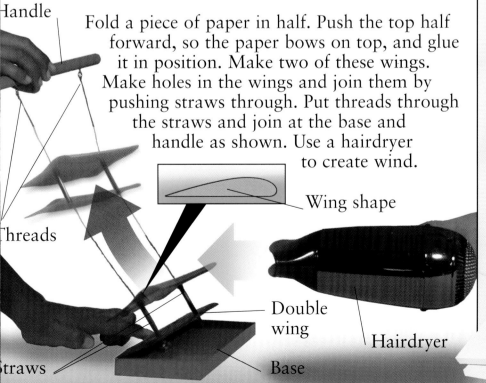

Double wing

Hairdryer

Base

Straws

How it WORKS

As air passes over the wing, it has farther to travel on the more-curved upper surface compared to the flat lower surface. It moves faster and has less pressure compared to the slower air passing under the lower side. The higher air pressure below pushes the wing upward.

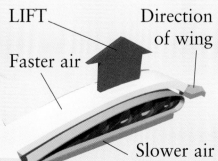

LIFT

Direction of wing

Faster air

Slower air

Newton's first law says that, unless a moving object is pushed or pulled by a force, it tends to keep going–in a straight line. So, when an object moves in a curved path, forces must be at work.

Earth's gravity pulls on the Moon with exactly enough force to make it curve around in a never-ending orbit. Any more force and the Moon would crash into Earth.

CIRCULAR MOTION

Things move in circles, along curves, and around corners all the time. To make them do so, a force must push or pull them from the side; otherwise, they would keep going straight. For the Moon and satellites orbiting the Earth, this force is the Earth's gravity. For a train, this force comes from the curve of the track pressing against the edges, or flanges, of the wheels. For a car turning a corner, this force comes from the angle of the tires and their grip with the road.

Like turning cycle wheels (left), gyroscopes have more inertia the faster they spin. You can feel it as resistance to change in position or movement.

As wheels spin faster, they are harder to tilt or tip to the side. It's easier to balance a faster bicycle than a slow one.

TWO FORCES

When an object is swung around in a circle on string, there seems to be a force pulling the string outward from the center. This is called centrifugal force. It results from the object trying to go in a straight line. In return, the string exerts a pull on the object to make it change direction continuously and move in a circle. This is called centripetal force.

On a merry-go-round ride, the people are flung outward by centrifugal force, but they are prevented from flying off by the centripetal force, which acts through the chains.

How it WORKS

As the lighter object twirls faster, creating a greater centrifugal force, the string must exert an increasing pull on it, as centripetal force, to keep it moving in a circle. Finally, the cork goes fast enough to overcome the pull of gravity on the heavier object and lifts it.

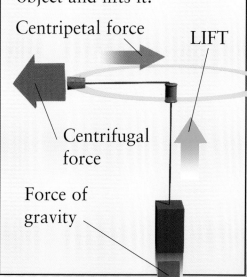

Centripetal force

LIFT

Centrifugal force

Force of gravity

HOW SPIN CAN LIFT

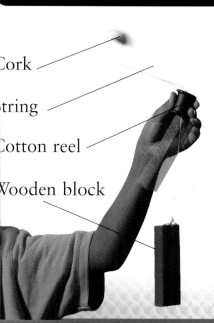

Cork

String

Cotton reel

Wooden block

Centrifugal force increases with an object's mass and speed. To show this, you need a cotton reel, a cork, and a wooden block and string.

Thread the string through the cotton reel. Tie the cork to one end and the block to the other end. Hold the reel upright and the block slides down, pulling the cork to the top of the reel. Start to twirl or spin the cork around.

19

Very few substances are totally solid and rigid. Under huge forces, even steel and rock are deformable, which means they can be squashed or stretched. But if the force is too great–CRACK!

DESIGNED TO DEFORM

Some materials easily deform, or change shape, when subjected to a force–and return, or recoil, to their original shape when the force is removed. Rubbers, elastics, and soft plastics can be flexed (bent), compressed (squeezed), and elongated (stretched). Foaming, or adding gas bubbles, increases their deformability.

A spring balance uses a spring to measure an object's weight.

The kinetic energy of the pole vaulter's body bends the pole, which then has stored energy. As the pole recoils, or regains its shape, it passes the energy back to the vaulter.

MORE FORCE, LONGER STRETCH

You can study how substances stretch according to the force on them by making a simple spring balance using a rubber band. Obtain a strong rubber band, string, a paper cup, a wooden board, a peg, paper, pens, and some weights. Hang the cup from the band. Fix a marker like a straw to the cup, and a strip of paper for the scale. With no weight in the cup, mark the cup's position. Put a small weight in the cup. The band stretches. Mark the position, then try heavier weights.

Peg

Rubber band

Paper cup

Marker

Scale

BEND, NOT BREAK

Deformable materials have thousands of uses, from squishy foam-plastic seat cushions to hard rubber engine mountings. Even metal parts of machines and structures are usually intended to deform and absorb some force, because if they tried to remain completely stiff, they might break under stress. A plane's wings are designed to flex up and down in high wind, rather than snap off!

How it **WORKS**

The force acting on the elastic band is Earth's gravity. It attracts each object in the cup according to its mass (the amount of matter in it). More mass means more gravitational pull, which stretches the band longer. For equal increases in weight, the band is stretched by equal amounts of length. This is known as Hooke's law, named after English scientist Robert Hooke (1635–1703). As the weights increase in equal amounts, the band may stretch slightly less each time. This shows that it is reaching its elastic limit and could break.

A clockwork mouse uses the stored energy from a coiled metal spring to move along. By winding it up, you transfer energy to the spring, to be released.

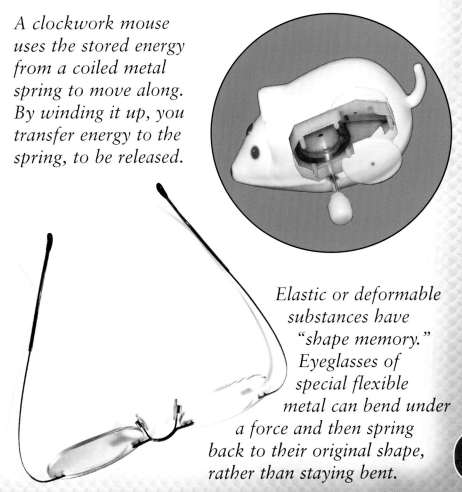

Elastic or deformable substances have "shape memory." Eyeglasses of special flexible metal can bend under a force and then spring back to their original shape, rather than staying bent.

We think of machines like bulldozers and cranes as complex devices with many moving parts. But in science, machines can be so simple that they hardly look like machines at all.

A stairway is really a simple machine, the inclined plane (slope). Climbing up a ladder takes lots of effort over a short distance. Stairs take less effort to climb, over a longer distance.

WHAT IS A MACHINE?

At the most basic level, a machine allows a smaller force or effort to overcome a larger one. This leads to another description of machines: They make work easier for us, or possible at all. You would not be able to jump to the top of a tall building. Yet the simplest machine of all can help you get there– a slope or ramp, known as the inclined plane.

"Spiral" staircases are simply slopes that are twisted around. They are useful because they use less space than straight stairs.

How it WORKS

A screw works on the same principle as a spiral staircase. The thread is a slope. When the screw is turned, the thread grips the surface and the screw moves downward.

Turning force

Thread

Downward force

MORE OF THE SIMPLEST

You cannot move a heavy rock with your hands, but you could with a simple machine: the lever. A lever is a rigid beam or rod that moves on a pivot called the fulcrum. It allows a smaller force, the effort, to overcome a larger one, the load.

A cantilever is a rigid beam or structure supported at one end only, like a diving board. It can even be a whole house. An entire section of this house is able to protrude beyond the cliff's edge by using the principle of levers to reduce stress.

There are three main orders of levers. You can compare the amount of effort required for each by making a simple wooden frame with holes in it, so that you can switch the positions of the fulcrum (F), load (L), and effort (E).

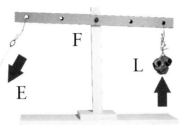

First order
The fulcrum is between the effort and the load. Examples are crowbars and pliers.

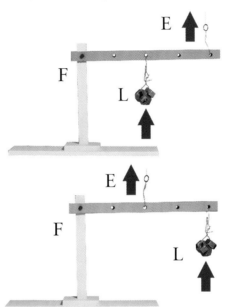

Second order
The load is between the fulcrum and the effort. Examples are wheelbarrows and nutcrackers.

Third order
The effort is between the fulcrum and the load. Examples are tongs and a straight arm.

How it WORKS

Using first and second order levers, you can apply greater force to an object using less effort. However, the force of the effort has to move much farther than the load is moved.

Third order levers require more effort since the effort is between the fulcrum and the load. Levers do not give you "something for nothing," but they make a job easier by dividing it into more manageable stages.

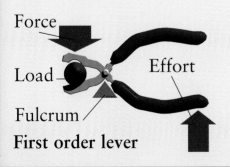

First order lever

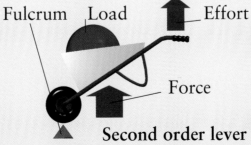

Second order lever

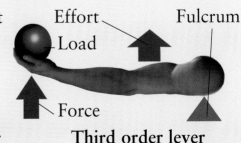

Third order lever

Giant wheels make it possible for us to move heavy loads that could not be pulled along the ground.

Some machines have parts that move straight along or to and fro. Other parts go round and round–rotary motion. The basis of spinning or rotating equipment is another very simple machine– the wheel and axle.

How it **WORKS**

A wheel can be described as being made up of lots of tiny inclined planes, all joined together to make a continuous slope. The forces involved as the wheel rolls along are exactly the same as those that apply to slopes (see page 22).

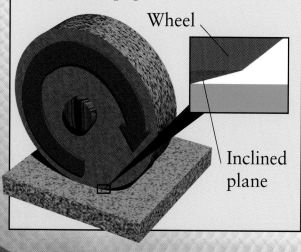

Wheel

Inclined plane

ENDLESS SLOPE

The wheel is a version of the simplest machine of all: the inclined plane (ramp or slope). A wheel is like an inclined plane wrapped around in a circular shape, so that its slope continues endlessly. Wheels spin or rotate on bars called axles. They enable loads to roll along, rather than be dragged, which causes great friction.

Water turning a big wheel provides a large rotating force on the axle, which, in turn, creates power to drive mills to grind flour.

Many designs of pulley blocks are used in factories, on cranes, on construction sites, and at ship docks—wherever heavy loads need to be lifted.

PULLEYS

The pulley is a wheel with raised edges or flanges, into which fits a length of rope, cable, or flexible belt made from plastic or rubber. Pulleys can be used to change the direction of a pulling force, as on a crane. Cranes usually have groups of pulleys called blocks, where the cable goes up and down between several pulleys. This works like a lever, so that a smaller force can be used to lift a larger load.

How it WORKS

Pulleys work rather like levers, as "force magnifiers." A small force can move a large mass or weight, but not very far. As more pulleys in each block are used, the force needed becomes less, but so does the height that the weight lifts. So, the small force has to be applied for a longer time. Overall, there is not "something for nothing." The pulley system makes the task easier, but also makes it take longer.

SIMPLE PULLEY SYSTEM

Make pulley blocks out of card, using a dowel as the axle. Attach cord to the top pulley and thread it around the lower pulley and back up around the top one. Hook a weight to the lower pulley. A friend holds the upper pulley while you pull on the cord. Now try attaching the weight directly to the cord when it is threaded through the top pulley only. Does this make it easier or more difficult?

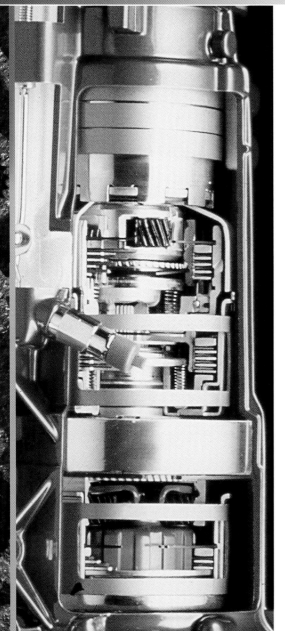

Could you cycle up a steep hill in top gear? Probably not—you could not push the pedals hard enough to get moving. Bottom or low gears are for going up hills, and top or high gears for coming down.

COGS AND TEETH

A gear or cog wheel has sharp "teeth" around its rim. These fit into or mesh with another gear wheel, so that a turning force, called torque, is transmitted from one to the other. Sets of gears, as rows or "chains" and gearing systems,

A car gearbox has many different cogs, which slide along on shafts and mesh together in different combinations for the various gears.

are used in many kinds of bicycles, cars, and other vehicles, and in hundreds of different types of motors and machinery.

How it **WORKS**

Gears can alter the direction of rotation and change rotational into linear (straight) movement. Basic transfer gears change rotation from counter-clockwise to clockwise. Bevel gears change the angle of rotation by 90°. Rack and pinion gears change rotation into linear movement.

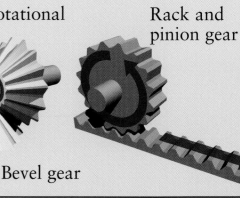

Rack and pinion gear

Basic transfer gear

Bevel gear

MORE FORCE, LESS SPEED

Gears are like levers and pulleys. They can change a turning force from small to large, but with a reduction in turning capacity. The change depends on a comparison of the number of teeth on each gear wheel, called the gear ratio. If the drive gear (with the driving or turning force) has 25 teeth, and the driven gear (which is turned) has 50, then the driven gear will turn at half the speed of the drive gear, but with twice the force. Or the reverse can happen.

Mechanical clocks have very precise transfer gears driven by a spring to move the hands at the correct rate.

Mountain bikers change gear often. This means, despite different angles of slopes and ups and downs, their legs always pedal at the same speed, which is the most efficient rate.

How it **WORKS**

With a suitable gear ratio, gears can change a small turning force into a large one. However, this also involves changing a fast turning speed into a slow one. This gear ratio is the type used by cyclists when they want to pedal up a hill. The pedals have to rotate more for the bicycle to cover the same distance. It will take longer, but will make it easier for the cyclist.

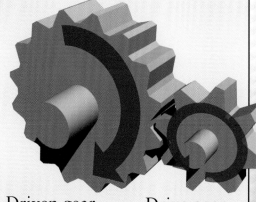

Driven gear   Drive gear

MORE FOR LESS, LESS FOR MORE

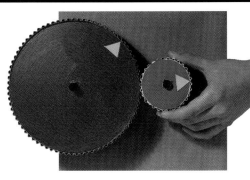

Gear ratios can be shown with a simple pair of gears. You need some strong card and some corrugated card, with ridges to make the gear teeth. Mark a point on the gears with arrows.

Spin the larger one as the drive gear. See how the smaller driven gear turns faster. Now turn the smaller one as the drive gear. See how the larger driven gear turns more slowly.

Pressure is a pressing, squeezing, or crushing force acting over a certain area. Light pressures can hardly be felt on the skin, while huge pressures can squash a car into a solid block.

The deeper you go into the ocean, the greater the water pressure. This is why deep-sea divers wear pressurized suits.

HELPFUL PRESSURE

Pressure is felt all the way through a volume of liquid, such as water or oil in a pipe. This feature is used in hydraulic equipment. In a water-filled pipe, the pressure of a pushing force at one end is felt all the way along and at the other end. So, forces can be transmitted long distances through pipes and tubes–which is why, when you turn on a kitchen faucet, water pours out.

There is air pressure all around us. It comes from the great weight of the layer of gases around the Earth, called the atmosphere. A barometer measures air pressure. Barometers are useful because air pressure changes with the wind and weather.

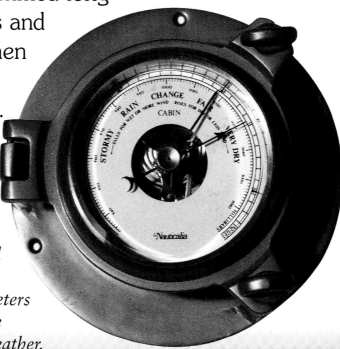

ROTTERDAM

MORE PRESSURE

Hydraulic machines can increase pressure, working in a similar way to levers and pulleys. Suppose a certain force is put on the liquid at one end of a pipe. The same force is felt at the other end, but if the other end is narrower, the pressure there will be greater, as the same force spreads over a smaller area. Machines use this area difference to increase pressure hundreds or thousands of times. However, if this huge pressure moves an object, the object will not travel very far, in the same way that a crowbar lifts a rock only a small amount.

Bulldozers, diggers, and dump trucks rely on hydraulic pressure. This is transferred by special oil inside very thick-walled tubing, which resists the great force. The pressure pushes pistons attached by rods to the moving parts.

How it WORKS

Hydraulic machines have a master cylinder and a slave cylinder. When pressure is applied to the master cylinder, the piston is pushed downward, pushing the hydraulic fluid along the tube to the slave cylinder. If the master cylinder has less area than the slave cylinder, then the slave cylinder will apply a stronger force but over a shorter distance. This is how hydraulic brakes work in cars.

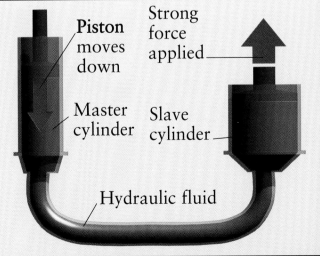

Piston moves down

Strong force applied

Master cylinder

Slave cylinder

Hydraulic fluid

MEASURING FORCES

The international unit of force is the newton (N). One newton is the force needed to make an object with a mass of 2.2 pounds (1 kg) increase in speed, or accelerate, by 3.3 feet (1m) per second every second. Some examples below show the forces needed to:

- Lift a medium apple   1 N
- Lift a quart carton of juice   10 N
- Push a broken-down car   700 N
- Power a jumbo jet   700,000 N
- Put a space shuttle into orbit   7.5 million N

The unit of the newton is really a vector quantity, which means that it has not only size or magnitude, but also direction.

FORCE AND "WEIGHT"

"Weight" is not a proper scientific term. When we measure the weight of an object, like our own body, what we are really measuring is force–the force of Earth's gravity pulling it downward. This gravitational force, g, is 4.457 N per pound at the Earth's surface. For a person with a mass of 110 pounds (50 kg), this force would be 490 N. However, weighing scales have numbers that "assume" the force in newtons is being divided by Earth's gravity, so they show the mass of an object in pounds. A person would lose consciousness if subjected to forces greater than about 8–9 g.

FORCE AND MASS

Mass is very different from weight. It is the amount of matter in an object or substance. An object with the mass of 2.2 pounds (1 kg) weighs 2.2 pounds here on Earth. It would still have a mass of 2.2 pounds if it were on the Moon or Sun, but its weight there would be very different, as suggested on the right. Mass is correctly measured by inertia–that is, how quickly the mass of an object accelerates

when subjected to a certain force. However, for practical purposes, it is usually defined by a metal bar made of platinum and iridium, which has the mass of exactly 2.2 pounds (1 kg). This special bar is kept in Sèvres, France, at the International Bureau of Weights and Measures.

MOMENTUM

The momentum of an object is its mass multiplied by its velocity or speed. If the mass is m pounds and the velocity is v feet per second, then:

- Momentum $M = m \times v$.

This measurement is in pounds-feet per second, which can be simplified to newton-seconds, N s. Examples are:

- Running mouse   0.05 N s
- Human sprinter   800 N s
- Truck on highway   1 million N s
- Cruising jumbo jet   100 million N s

THE FORCE OF GRAVITY

All objects exert gravitational pull, but it depends on their mass (amount of matter), so we usually notice it only with truly huge objects like planets. The gravitational pull at the Earth's surface, 4.457 N per pound, is known as g, or the "g force." Compared to this, examples of gravitational pulls in other places are:

- Surface of the Moon   0.16 g
- Surface of planet Jupiter   2.4 g
- Surface of the Sun   27 g
- On a neutron star   140 billion g

A person who weighs 100 pounds on Earth weighs (100 x 0.16) = 16 pounds on the Moon.

GLOSSARY

airfoil
Structure or wing-shape with the upper surface more curved than the lower one. The difference in air flow over the two surfaces provides the force known as lift.

elastic
An object or substance that changes shape, or deforms, when subjected to a force, but then returns, or recoils, back to its original shape when the force is removed.

energy
An ability to cause change or make something happen. Energy has many different forms, such as electricity, sound, heat, light, motion, and chemicals.

force
A push or pull that can change the movement or the shape of an object. Forces are measured in units called newtons (see opposite).

friction
Rubbing or scraping as surfaces or substances move past each other, usually generating heat.

gravity
The force that pulls two objects toward each other, no matter what their size.

kinetic energy
Energy possessed by an object or substance because of its motion or movement. For example, wind is moving air and has kinetic energy.

lever
A rigid beam or rod that turns at a pivot (the fulcrum). It is a simple machine that allows a smaller force (the effort) to overcome a larger one (the load).

pressure
The amount of force pushing on a given area. It is measured in newtons per unit of area–for example, newtons per square foot.